MW01274029

The Magical Journey of Life

DAVID T.D. NUNN

Copyright © 2024 David T.D. Nunn
All rights reserved.
ISBN: 9798324109226

This book is enchanted just for you.
It will guide you through your
Magical Journey of Life.

Once upon a time, in a world filled with twinkling stars and spinning planets, there was a curious question that danced through the minds of creatures big and small.

It was a question that whispered in the rustling leaves, giggled in the babbling brooks, and soared through the vast skies.

"What is our purpose?" wondered the little creatures as they scurried and fluttered about.

One wise owl, with feathers as soft as moonlight, decided to embark on a journey to discover the answer.

After his great adventure he gathered all the animals in the enchanted forest to share the secret.

"The answer," said the wise owl, "is as simple as the song of the crickets on a summer night."

"All it takes is the magic of looking back in time and connecting the dots of our incredible journey."

He began to tell the tale when the universe burst into existence like a dazzling firework in the cosmic sky.

From that magical explosion, the universe set forth on an incredible adventure, creating the tiniest building blocks on the world's biggest canvas.

As the journey continued, it led to the creation of wondrous things like stars, planets, and eventually, to the most extraordinary beings of all – us!

"Before we were wise and clever, like you all are now, we were like the playful animals of the forest, reacting to the world around us," the wise owl continued.

"Our purpose, my dear friends, is the fantastic progress we've made along the way!"

The animals listened intently as the owl explained that progress was like following a trail of footprints through the forest. Every step, from the tiniest to the grandest, is part of the magical journey.

"But then," the owl hooted, "we were given a special gift called choice. With choice, we could decide the path we wanted to take."

The wise owl smiled warmly, "if you choose the magical journey, the key is to do everything with your whole heart, reaching your full potential and helping others do the same. If you choose a different path, that's perfectly okay too."

As the moonlight shimmered through the leaves, the wise owl shared his final wish, "may each of you embark on your own amazing adventure while spreading love to yourself and all the friends you meet along the way."

And so, under the twinkling stars and the watchful eyes of the wise owl, the enchanted forest echoed with the joyful laughter of creatures determined to make their own mark on The Magical Journey of Life.

Now, get ready to embark on your Magical Journey of Life!

About the Author

David tries to pet every dog he sees. He is a first time author and lives in the Pacific Northwest with his loving family. He studied art history at the University of British Columbia and architecture at Harvard's Graduate School of Design. He was inspired to write a story about finding one's purpose when searching for his own. He hopes this book can lead others towards a magical life full of progress and love.

Manufactured by Amazon.ca
Acheson, AB

13355484R00026